FRANZ JOSEPH HAYDN

CONCERTO

for Violin and Orchestra / für Violine und Orchester

No. 1
C Major / C-Dur

Hob. VIIa:1

Edited and supplied with cadenzas by
Herausgegeben und mit Kadenzen versehen von

Carl Flesch

Edition for Violin and Piano
Ausgabe für Violine und Klavier

EIGENTUM DES VERLEGERS · ALLE RECHTE VORBEHALTEN
ALL RIGHTS RESERVED

EDITION PETERS

LONDON · FRANKFURT/M. · LEIPZIG · NEW YORK

Fatto per il Luigi Tomasini

KONZERT IN C DUR

Joseph Haydn
Bearbeitet und mit Kadenzen versehen
von Carl Flesch
Klavierauszug von Wilhelm Scholz

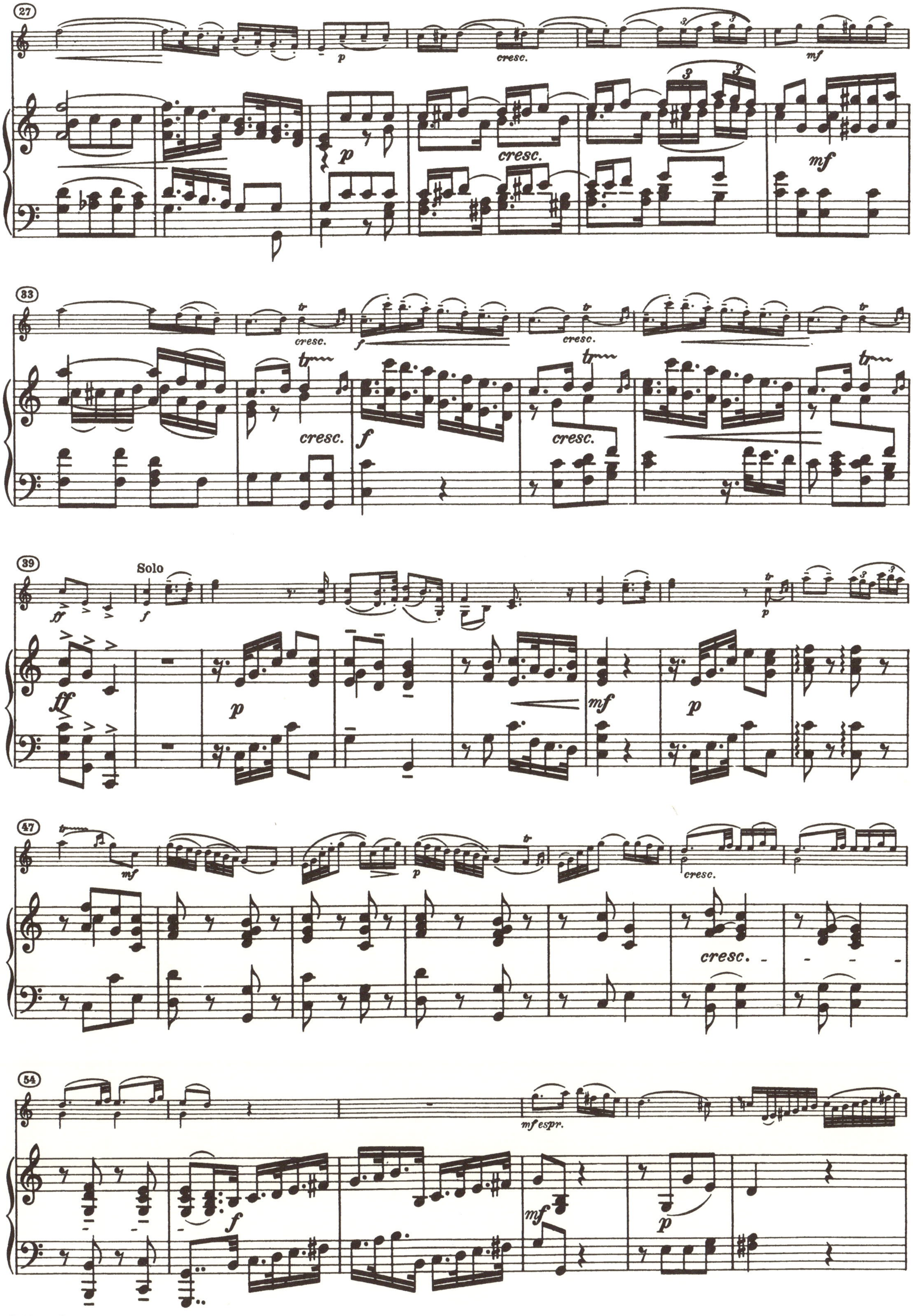
27
cresc.
mf
33
cresc.
39
Solo
47
54
mf espr.

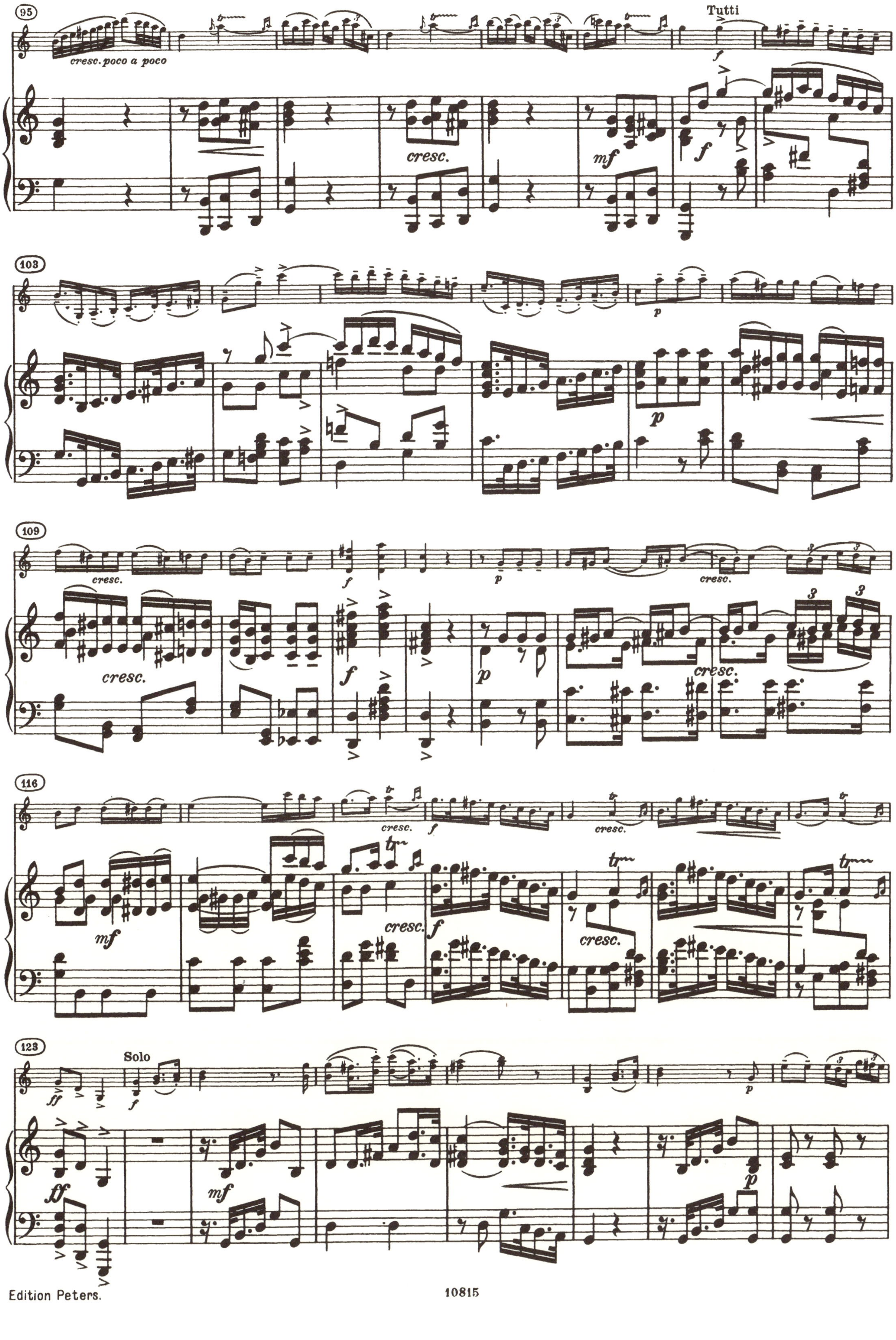
95
cresc. poco a poco
Tutti
cresc.
103
109
cresc.
116
cresc.
123
Solo

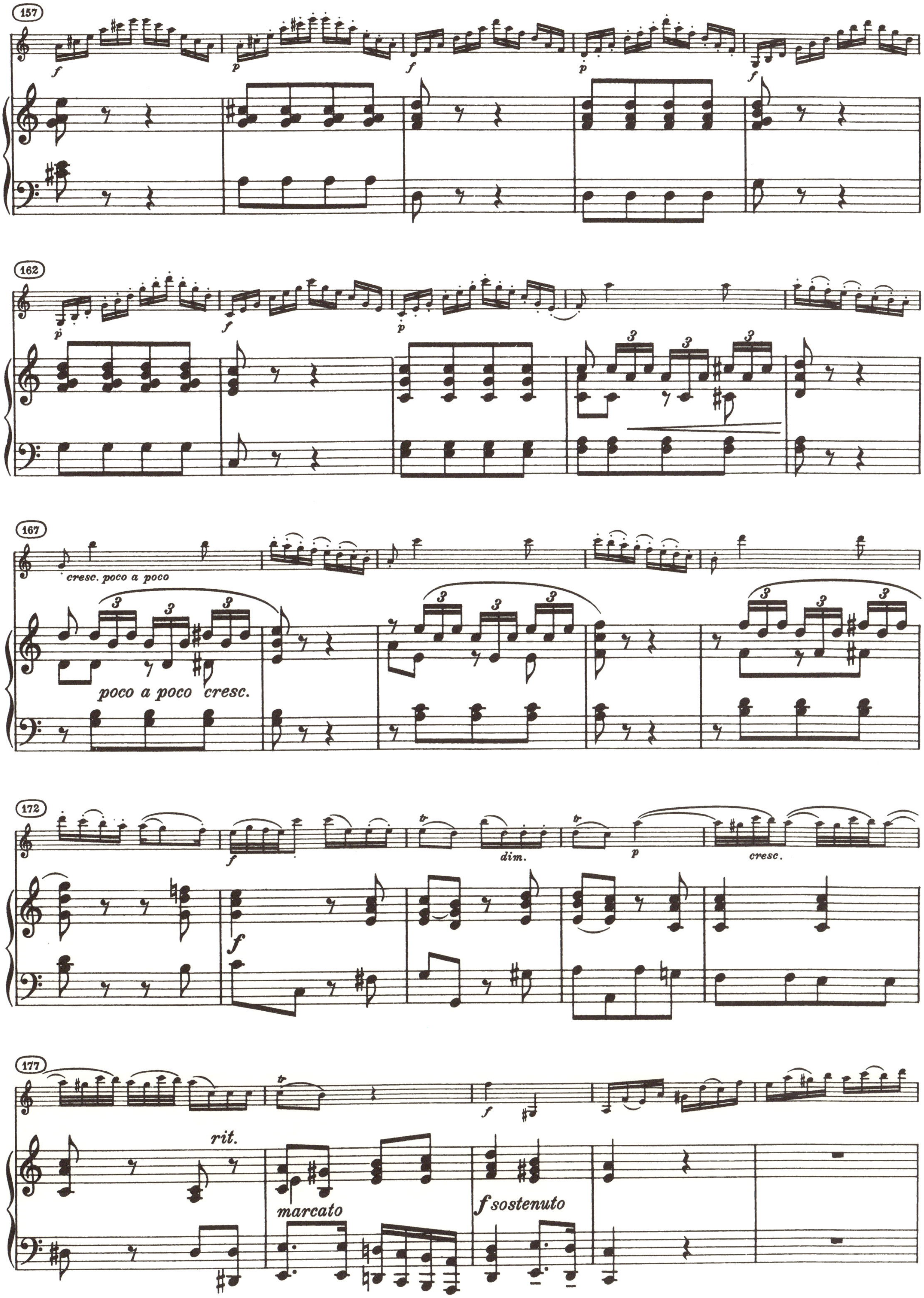
157
162
167
cresc. poco a poco
poco a poco cresc.
172
dim.
cresc.
177
rit.
marcato
f sostenuto

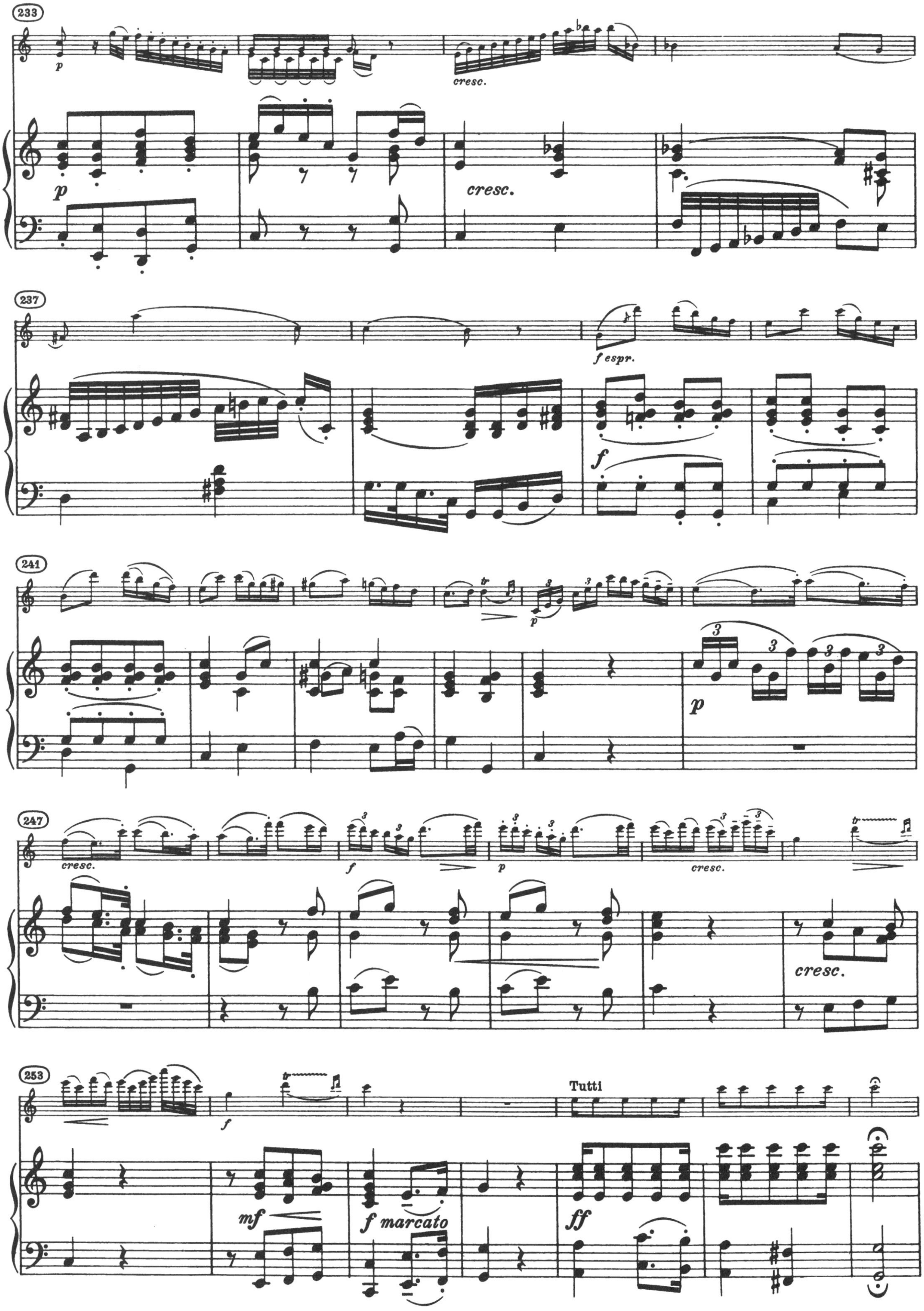
233
p
cresc.
237
f espr.
f
241
p
247
cresc.
mf
f marcato
253
Tutti
ff

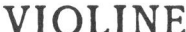

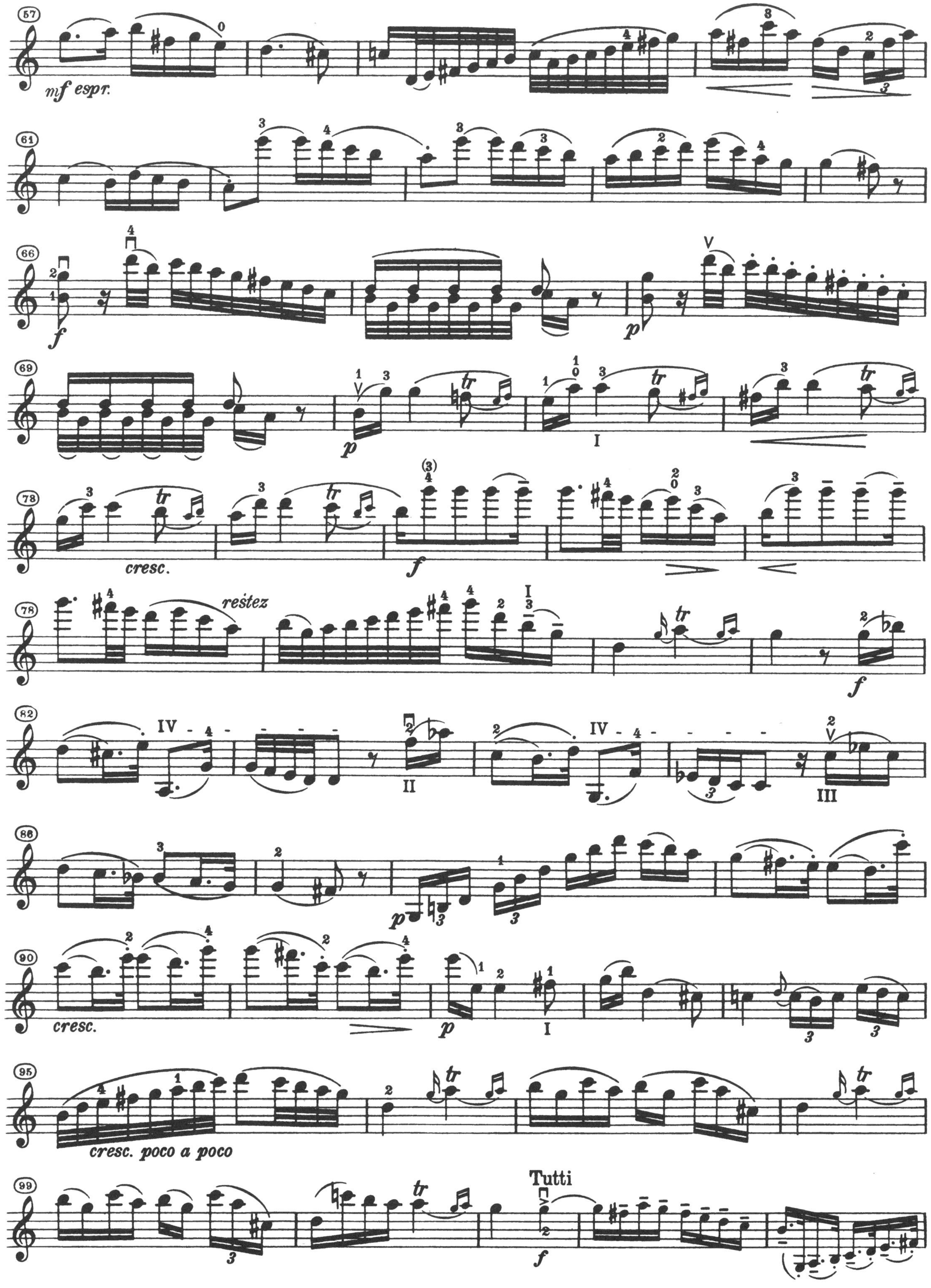
mf espr.
cresc.
restez
cresc. poco a poco
Tutti

VIOLINE

VIOLINE

VIOLINE

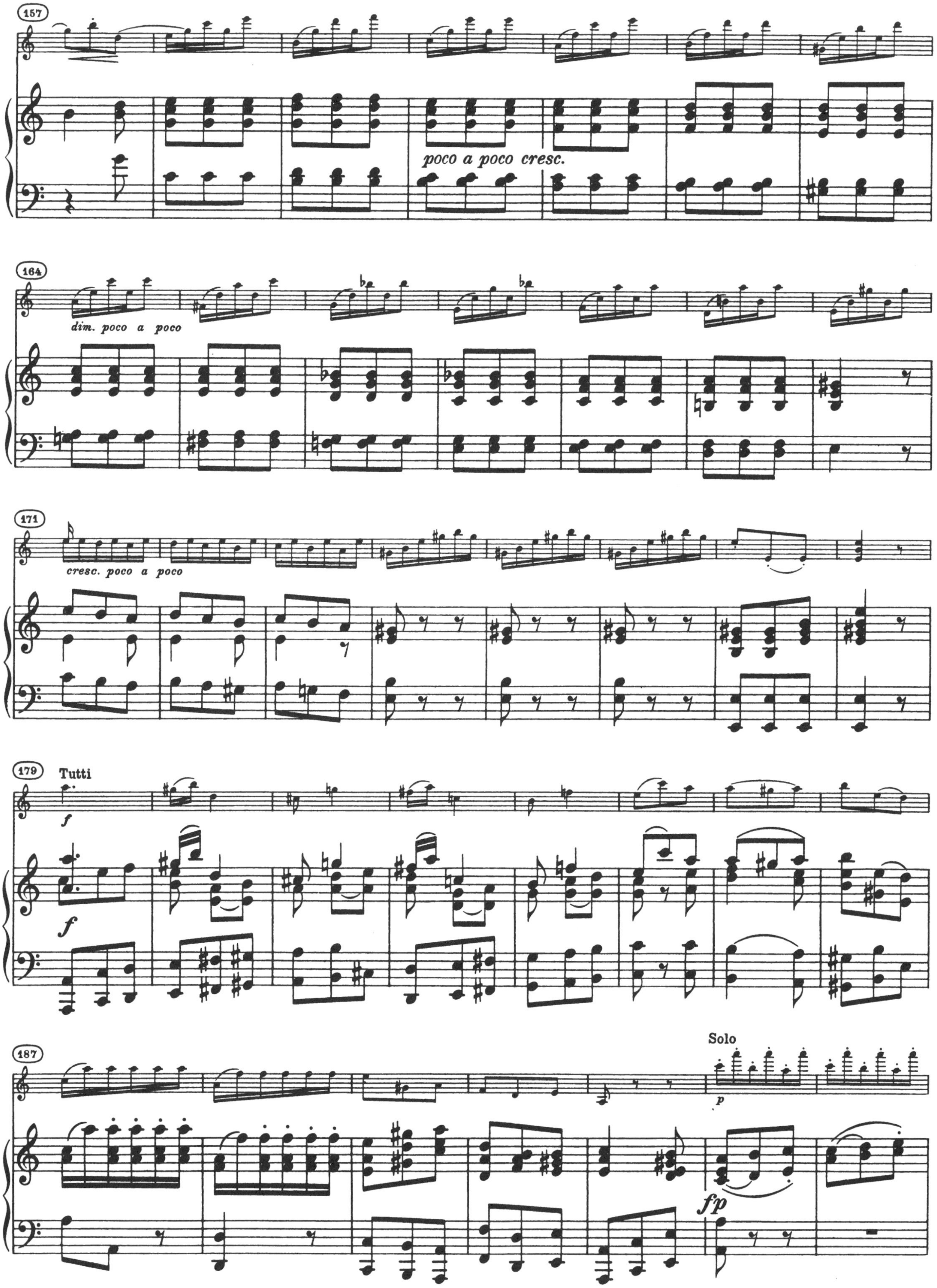
157
poco a poco cresc.
164
dim. poco a poco
171
cresc. poco a poco
179
Tutti
f
f
187
Solo
p
fp